bush
PUBLISHING
& associates

ENTREPRENEUR

ROAD MAP FOR SUCCESS

JOSH C. JONES

bush
PUBLISHING
& associates

ENTREPRENEUR: ROAD MAP FOR SUCCESS

ISBN: 978-1-944566-27-2 (PAPERBACK)
ISBN: 978-1-944566-28-9 (ebook)

Printed in the United States of America.

First printing 2021 by Bush Publishing and Associates, LLC
Tulsa, Oklahoma
www.bushpublishing.com

Bush Publishing & Associates, LLC books may be ordered at bookstores everywhere and at Amazon.com.

Cover Art, Layout and Design by Bush Publishing and Associates, LLC, Tulsa, OK.

Editing by Jocelyne Hankins.

All opinions expressed in this book are the author's.

Dedicated to Grampy

(Philip W. Wilson)

Thank you for leading by example.

I love you!

TABLE OF CONTENTS

ACKNOWLEDGMENTS

"A clever way to be quoted is to quote yourself."
– Josh C. Jones

A wise man once said, "A clever way to be quoted is to quote yourself." So this is what I did, I quoted myself. Does that mean I am a wise man if I said so myself?

Anywho.

Writing this book was a five year process of research, difficult and wonderful crushing and molding experiences in each characteristic, and a tremendous hill climbed for myself.

No one is required to thank anyone else for any help, but a good, honest, and thankful person understands the importance and value of gratitude and respect; and that such accolades are endowed upon them and those they acknowledge. Besides, I would not be a good entrepreneur if I did not give credit where credit was due (read on, and you will see what I mean).

So, with that said, let's get on with the acknowledgments. Shall we?

I would like to thank God first and foremost. Without Him, I would not be here, nor would I have been able to do anything. Without God, I would never have had the opportunities and experiences in life that have allowed me to learn and grow in each of these characteristics. Without Him, I could not have written this book with the knowledge, clarity, and creativity I have. I owe everything to God, and I thank Him for it all.

To my family:

Thank you, Leonard R. Jones. Thank you, Dad, for your input on my rough draft. I greatly appreciate you taking the time to read it, marking it up with notes, and thoroughly answering the question sheet I sent to you. Your responses about the way it was written encouraged me to make the corrections you mentioned, continue the hard work of writing this book, take the risk of publishing it, and face the fear of any potential negative outcome. I love you, Dad!

Thank you, Judy B. Jones. Thank you, Mom, for encouraging me to write and for all the walks we took discussing different ideas, worries, and insights, and passing inspiration back and forth. I love you, Mom!

Thank you, Christopher R. P. Jones. Thank you, brother, for joining me on some of my ventures, and I thank you for allowing me to accompany you on some of yours. The insights obtained and lessons learnt helped in the creation of this book. I love you, brother!

Thank you, Philip W. Wilson. Thank you, Grampy, for your love and encouragement with my writings. The ramblings we shared, and even the intelligent conversations we had, all helped me better understand certain concepts I had yet to put two and two together on. Your request for the first copy of this book, when published (after reading the rough draft), spoke volumes about the content, readability, and belief in the success of this book, for myself, and the help it could provide others. You truly are a wealth of wisdom, and I thank God for every moment we get to spend together. I love you, Grampy!

To my friends: Ryan Brandt, Rick Luttrell, Sean Johnston

Thank you, Ryan, for working with me all these years. I am glad we are friends. Our ability to keep each other motivated and encouraged while working on projects (and especially in certain meetings) has helped greatly in acquiring the knowledge and understanding needed for the writing of this book. I look forward to all the future projects we will get to work on together. Also, thank you for traveling down that entrepreneur journey with me with Two Titans Media L.L.C. (it may be on hold, for now, but it is not over yet…we think). That venture with TTM made for a great story about hard work.

Thank you, Rick, for allowing me to join you and help you on your journey to creating a podcast of which I was one of the producers, creative designers, and audio engineers. [Update: Unfortunately, between the initial writing of this book's first rough draft and the final editing for publication, this podcast has been discontinued. It was still a great journey full of learning and growth for all of us.]

Thank you, Sean, for bringing me and Ryan on board with your short screenplay, *Commitment,* all those long years ago. The struggles, hardships, and revelation of (or apparent absence of) some characteristics, while making that short film, really did strengthen all of our friendships, as it truly did take us to task on some life lessons—well, I know it did for me. I thank you, and I am glad we are friends.

1

PROLOGUE

"A person who sees a problem is a human being; a person
who finds a solution is visionary; and the person who goes
out and does something about it is an entrepreneur."[1]

– Naveen Jain

Imagine with me, if you will, a tranquil island with a warm but
pleasant tropical breeze. You are sitting back in a lawn chair,
barefoot, drinking your favorite cold drink, while the tropical breeze
blows across your face. It feels warm from the sun shining down its
brilliant rays upon your face, yet cool with a little bit of ocean spray
from the emerald colored waves gently beating the shore. You bury
your feet and curl your toes in the white sand, and immediately a
sensation of freedom and relaxation enters your body. The sand tickles
your feet; it grips to your form; it wraps its massaging particles around
your feet and hugs your sole.

In this serene place, there is no worry, no stress, no frustration.

This place is pure relaxation; it is pure bliss.

This is the true life of the successful—of the entrepreneur.

Entrepreneur! That fantastic title in life that allows one to buy a big house on the coastal front of any state or country they want, afford whatever their heart desires, and sit back and relax on the beach, in the sun, with a cold drink in one hand and a phone in the other; the phone, of course, is how the entrepreneur is able to do their job anywhere in the world and make millions of dollars doing what they want, whenever they want.

This is usually what we think of when we hear the word "entrepreneur," right? Financial wealth, complete freedom, total control, the ability to be our own boss. Well, if not that, then something very similar in regard to wealth, freedom, and relaxation, I'm sure.

Entrepreneurs are people who control their own life, their own work schedule, their own pay, their own vacation time, their own retirement. Aren't they? This was what I believed, and one of the reasons why I originally wanted to be an entrepreneur. In the words of William Wallace, from the movie *Braveheart*, "Freeeedomm!"[2] So, this assessment is correct then, right?

Well, yes and no. It can be for some who embark on this journey, just as it can be for some who never venture into the entrepreneur life. One does not need to be an entrepreneur to have wealth or to be successful. The privileges and outcome to any journey depend on the results of choices made, lifestyles lived, and futures invested in.

So, what is an entrepreneur then, and why would one want to try to be one?

An entrepreneur, according to Merriam-Webster, is known as "one who organizes, manages, and assumes the risks of a business or enterprise."[3] That must mean they should be a business owner, CEO, or a full investor in an enterprise, right? Maybe. That is one interpretation. But is this all an entrepreneur is? Is this all it means when one says "entrepreneur"—an investor or manager who tends to own their own business? I would dare say, no; it means so much more. I think the word "entrepreneur" carries many connotations: owner, inventor, writer, innovator, risk-taker, go-getter, leader; the list could go on.

To me, an entrepreneur is one who steps out of the ordinary, out of their comfort zone, to take great personal and financial risk in the hope of generating wealth and happiness and, hopefully, recurring monies for the advancement of themselves, their income, their happiness, and their life in order to provide a better future for not just themselves, but others as well; they do this by working on, or toward, their passion or desire—work they enjoy performing every day.

Woah. Hold on. Be like a barbell and wait. (I know, that was a stretch for a pun.)

Seriously though, hold on a moment. That sounds kind of selfish. If an entrepreneur is working to advance their own income, wealth, happiness, and, well, life, then they are focusing on themselves. To focus on yourself is selfish, isn't it? That would mean entrepreneurs are selfish individuals, right?

Well, let me answer that question this way: Do you try to work more hours, or more jobs (side-hustles) to make higher wages and to increase your income, wealth and happiness, and, well, life?

To be selfish is to be concentrated, or totally focused, on oneself without any consideration for any other person; a selfish person seeks to advance themselves at the expense of, and with disregard to, another.

We all have bills to pay. We all have basic survival needs to be met. Some of us might even have a family to feed and support. We all have that same basic need to ensure our own personal survival and our future, whether we state that need is driven by a desire to, hopefully, improve the life of another or not; it is still a need for self-survival and to better ourselves.

A good person, entrepreneur or not, is not so driven by their own desires that they selfishly disregard another's well-being just to advance their own. However, it is very difficult to help other people in this way—income, wealth, happiness, success—when we ourselves are in need and unstable.

It is almost inevitable that each of us will, at some point in life, find ourselves in those difficult times of need, and when we do, we will seek out inspiration, motivation, and hope, in the world and from others during those times to help us survive. We all will, hopefully, find ourselves surviving those difficult times and then telling our stories of inspiration, motivation, and hope to others. However, if we do not choose to take care of ourselves first, then we will exponentially decrease our chances to pull ourselves out of whatever pit we might find ourselves in, and we will less likely be in a firm and positive position to help our family, our friends, strangers, or anyone who needs inspiration, motivation, or hope. No one can help us if we are not first willing to accept help, put on our work boots, and choose to also help ourselves.

So, helping ourselves is a good thing because our stories of perseverance, grit, hard work, and hope, can help lift others to another level of happiness, courage, wealth, and hope in their lives through inspiration and information; but those stories are not published while we are in need (while we are still in those times of difficulty), they are still being written. Remember, it is the end story that we endured and how we survived those times of need that truly helps others. As the late Hollywood actress, Audrey Hepburn, once said, "Remember, if you ever need a helping hand, it's at the end of your arm; as you get older, remember you have another hand: The first is to help yourself, the second is to help others."[4]

There is nothing wrong with wanting to better our own life through gaining finances, to better our own life by increasing our status, wealth, and happiness. It is when we solely focus on ourselves, completely ignoring those around us, and attempt to gain this wealth, status, and happiness by "any means necessary," that the question and concern of selfishness, greed, ethics, and morality come into play. As John Wesley states in *The Works of the Reverend John Wesley, A.M.*, "Having, First, gained all you can, and, Secondly saved all you can, Then give all you can."[5]

By helping yourself, you are, in turn, better able to help others; and by helping others, you also help yourself.

So, being an entrepreneur is about pursuing your passions, your goals, and your dreams, so you can, hopefully, live a happier and better quality of life and, in turn, better help others.

2

AM I WORTH IT?

"Your net worth can fluctuate, but your self-worth should only appreciate."[1] – Chris Gardner

---

Anyone who is, or who has tried to be, an entrepreneur knows that this path is not an easy one. It is winding, usually unpaved, and full of potholes and detours. It is traversing unknown (to the entrepreneur at least) territories of physical, mental, and sometimes even spiritual, limits of business, life, and especially one's own self, and then, when those limits are fully reached and there seems to be no way to stretch those limits anymore, the entrepreneur still pushes further. In short, being an entrepreneur is no easy task.

It takes a lot from you.

It takes a lot out of you.

It takes a lot of you.

Entrepreneurship is not what we consider "a day job." It is not a regular nine to five; it is not always a set timetable for pay, vacation, or days and hours worked. In fact, an entrepreneur (such as those in the field of media and events as I was) is typically at the mercy of the client when it comes to a work schedule. However, the decision to be an entrepreneur can be, and most likely will be, a rewarding experience for anyone and everyone who decides to step out, take that journey, and strive for their own success.

Clear enough? Sometimes I make things as clear as wearing glasses in a sand storm while spraying those glasses, trying to clean them, at the very same time.

So, please, permit me to add some supplemental information here to help clear the mud I helped make that is now smeared on those glasses from spraying them in the sand storm. In other words, allow me to give you additional information here to clarify what I mean when I say "rewarding" and "own success."

When I say "rewarding," it does not always mean successful; rewarding is worthwhile, gratifying, advantageous. Rewarding increases the chances of success. Each opportunity and outcome are a rewarding learning experience to help us reach our success.

Rewarding is defined by Merriam-Webster as "yielding or likely to yield a reward," and as "serving as a reward."[2]

Though rewarding can be viewed as subjective, it is, in my opinion, more objective than subjective. It is objective in the sense that its second definition (serving as a reward) can be definitively argued and substantiated by the reward giver, even if it is not accepted by the reward receiver: for example, a kind word of gratitude, an exchange of goods or money, a smile, etc. It is subjective in the first definition relating to time; we must have hope and faith in the future, and we must be willing to perceive our actions and any outcome in a positive view. We must understand our power of acceptance and accept our time, work, ascension or lack thereof, and even our failures, as a positive opportunity to learn and grow. By doing so, we can greatly increase our chances of success, and this is rewarding.

Experience, positivity, optimism, steps forward—these are all rewarding.

Besides, success is a relative term and is subjective to the individual. What you see as success may greatly differ from what I see as success, and vice versa.

Allow me to give a quick example here:

John Doe and his wife, Jane Doe, see success as being rich. However, when each one defines what "rich" means to them, they may reveal different perceptions of "rich," thus creating a divergence in their views of success. To John, being rich means having a net worth of ten thousand dollars. His wife, Jane, however, sees being rich as having a net worth of two million dollars. At this moment, their net worth is 1.3 million dollars. To John, they are not only successful at being rich, they have also greatly exceeded their goal of success. However, to his wife, they are still unsuccessful.

All right. Much like the entrepreneur who might encounter roadblocks on his journey, we, too, must get off this detour and back on the main topic of this chapter—the entrepreneur.

To be an entrepreneur, it takes hard work, commitment, determination, hard work, persistence, perseverance, hard work, positivity, creativity, and hard work, just to name a few. I know, I said "hard work" four times. That's because it takes a lot of hard work. In the end though, it will all be worth it. At least, that is what we tell ourselves, right?

Absolutely. If we stay positive and work hard, we will not have any problems keeping our faith or hope of achieving our success as an entrepreneur, right? Always be positive. Yes, always try to be positive, but we are still human and, as humans, we must understand that doubt will inevitably creep in. Doubt, unfortunately, goes with negativity. And as I write in my book *Destiny: Life or Death, Choose Your Destiny*, "According to the same [scientific] article, nearly eighty percent of those thoughts are negative. Eighty percent of our thoughts are negative."[3] We can fight the negativity and doubt all we want but, much like a determined squatter, doubt will find its way to enter and occupy valuable space. When it does enter our mind, doubt will then invite fear to be its roommate. Fear will then bring negative thoughts and begin to write all over the walls of our mind, just like the character

Jack Torrance did in the movie *The Shining*[4]; the difference will be that fear will not write just one phrase over and over, it will fill the walls of our mind with many, many questions.

- Will it really be worth it in the end?

- Will I be able to do what is required of me as an entrepreneur?

- Am I skilled enough in my field?

- Am I good enough at all?

- Do I have enough money (am I wealthy enough at this point) to make this happen?

- Do I have the ability to make this happen?

- Will people like me?

- Will people like what I have to offer?

- What if I fail?

- Am I worth it?

All these questions have one important theme intertwined amongst them: **Self-Worth**.

Will you be able to do what is required of you to be an entrepreneur?

Well, the answer to that question is quite simple, and I can definitively say, 100%, without a shadow of doubt, that the answer is: "I do not know."

I can tell you that you are worth it, each of us are, but, ultimately, you must decide because only you can determine for yourself if you have what it takes to be an entrepreneur and if what it takes will be worth it in the end.

Remember, the success and rewards it can bring are relative to each individual and their perception of success. The rewards, both the successes and failures, will be inevitable and invaluable, but only if we choose to view them with an optimistic and positive attitude.

What I can tell you is that, for me, this journey has been worth it. Although I have had many more perceived failures than successes on my personal journey thus far, I truly believe the successes I have been honored and blessed to enjoy were only possible because of the lessons learned and opportunities presented because of the failures.

So, what have I done that gives me any insight or credit to discuss this topic? Excellent question. If you will, please allow me a few moments to give a brief explanation—not to brag or boast, but to give a little insight into my entrepreneurial journey.

I have been a freelance contractor in the media field for years. I have operated the camera, audio, and replay. I was the director, the gaffer (which is the chief electrician, the lighting guy), and the editor for various projects with various companies: my own of course, the NBA, the WNBA, music artists (local and professional), independent movies, Xtreme Fight Night (broadcasted on the UFC network), and college sports broadcasts, just to name a few. I have tried my hand at acting, and I was nominated for best leading actor in a feature film. I, along with my friend and business partner at the time, created an award-winning short film—the making of this film is its own motivational story of four years of perseverance, creativity, commitment, and, more importantly, a lot of hard work. I have worked in live theater (on stage and behind the scenes), and I have helped a few small businesses either get started or grow to higher levels. I am also a published author.

Through all this, throughout my time attempting to be an entrepreneur thus far, I have identified five characteristics that, in my opinion and understanding, are very important and common among those we might perceive as successful entrepreneurs.

These characteristics can be learned and applied by all of us (even if we do not plan to be entrepreneurs) if we are willing to attempt, sacrifice, work hard, and endure. These characteristics contain different aspects with important components that will help shape a person of good character as well.

It is worth noting: I have seen and worked with others who lacked one, or many, of these characteristics and, as frustrating as it can be sometimes, have still attained their idea of success. I have also witnessed many of these same individuals lose their grip on their success, some falling hard and losing much more than material gains because of a lack of one or more of these characteristics. I have noticed that it is those who not only attain their success but also are able to maintain it that possess these five characteristics; they are also the types of individuals people tend to enjoy being around and work with time and time again. Your success, much like your destiny, is your choice.

You might think of these characteristics as part of an individual's overall character. As John Wooden so perfectly put it, "Ability may get you to the top, but it takes character to keep you there."[5]

I am going to list these characteristics as MUST BE, because I think that they are musts.

3

LEADERSHIP

An Entrepreneur must be:

A (good) LEADER

He sat atop his golden chair, observing those who were commissioned to build him his empire. He had a distinction that set him apart from the front-line worker, which, as he interpreted for himself, was every person beneath his command, and this distinction meant he was in charge. His status made him appear superior; he held influence to ensure his demands were met; he had a white-knuckled grip on the power to punish any person who disobeyed; he had the corner office with the big window and the scenic view of the city; he felt like he was king; he was their leader!

A leader is one who, as the old clichéd version goes, silences, oppresses, and whips his employees, forcing them to meet his demands over harsh and demeaning conditions while sitting atop a golden chair carried by those same employees. I'm kidding, of course. This is not a leader. This is a despot, an oppressor. This is also what we so eloquently call a "bad leader." Do not be like this. Aspire to be a good leader.

Well then, who is a leader?

A leader is anyone who is in charge or who commands others, be it a group, country, class, organization, etc. Being in charge, however, has nothing to do with how a person leads, acts, or conducts oneself. How one decides to lead is what makes him or her a good leader or a bad leader.

So, a leader is a combination of multiple things. More importantly, though, a leader understands the vision and mission of the business or job: the purpose of and the procedure (or standards) by which the purpose gets fulfilled. In the case of an entrepreneur pursuing his own personal vision, the procedure (or standards) by which his vision gets accomplished will be determined by his foundational beliefs.

There are a few components within this characteristic that I believe are needed to be a good leader; you do not need them all in order to be a good leader, but if you wish to be a true leader, then I think all are a must.

Henceforth, when I write "leader," I am referring to a good leader, unless otherwise stated.

A leader is a mentor, teacher, trainer.

Simon Sinek says, "A leader's job is not to do the work for others; it's to help others figure out how to do it themselves, to get things done, and to succeed beyond what they thought possible."[2]

As leaders, we are meant to mentor and guide people on their journey while ensuring everyone stays on track with the vision of the business or job at hand. We, as leaders, should be willing to step into the trenches with those we are entrusted to guide, so they might better understand what the issue is, if there is one, and to work on solutions with them. In doing so, we are better able to guide everyone through any possible problems. As leaders, it is our responsibility to mentor those we have the honor to advise.

As leaders, we must understand that there is knowledge to be learned from everyone. We should know and accept that to be teachers means to impart our knowledge for the student to absorb while also helping the student see from a new perspective; we should also understand that, by doing so, we, in turn, have the opportunity to learn from the student both new knowledge and perspectives for our own life.

As leaders, we are to train those we are leading, so everyone understands the purpose and the vision of the business or job so that they will be ready to take the reins when we, the current leaders, are gone. Without training the next generation, we could become a relic, and we greatly increase the chances of the business (or job, or vision) faltering, and eventually crumbling. When the vision is ignored, the purpose changes; and when the purpose changes, the foundation laid and the sacrifices made become irrelevant; and when the foundation laid and the sacrifices made become irrelevant, the business (or job, or vision) will no longer exist as it was. Without this meekness (restrained power) by us, the leaders, to humble ourselves and to put others over our own career or desire for legacy by training them, the next generation, to be ready to carry the vision, our legacy, and the legacy of all those who came before us could very well be buried and forgotten in the sands of time.

As leaders, we are to mentor those we serve with guidance while we teach them the knowledge and skills we have learned to train the next generation to carry on the vision, and the purpose for what we have created or been commissioned to lead.

A leader understands the phrase "the buck stops here."

As leaders, we are expected to take responsibility for the final decisions made, failures seen, and successes achieved (or in the case of a business with employees, being a leader also means sharing the glory of the success). A leader is much like the director of a film—it does not matter who made the error causing the film to be received with low regard—be it bad audio, cinematography, acting, editing, or whatever went wrong with it—the director is the name mostly associated with the film that will receive the brunt, right or wrong, and they will be called upon for the error. This is because the director was in charge of bringing all aspects together and successfully fulfilling the vision. As leaders, we must understand and accept this responsibility. We also should know that it is our job to protect our people and, if necessary, discipline those who made an error (in private preferably and if possible), and help them learn from the error so it will not be repeated. When we conduct ourselves as leaders should and protect our people, they will, in turn, reciprocate by helping protect us.

As leaders, we should share success with everyone on our team. We must understand that, even if we appear to be alone on this entrepreneurial journey, we are not truly alone. To be technical about it, and in reality, we did not achieve anything without the help of others and, in this realization, when applicable, we give credit where credit is due when success is achieved.

The auteur, who is a filmmaker, or creative artist, who had significant creative input in a project (typically a movie) and is often regarded as the author, had the help of the cast and possibly the crew of the film. The solo business owner had the help of the clients and other creative businesses in getting his services or goods to the clients: the website company, business card prints, etc. The solo music artist had his teachers (if he took lessons), friends, family, and earliest fans and critics to help him build his skills and better grow as a musician. The book author had the help of those who came before him, those on whom he bounced ideas off, and those who gave feedback on the rough drafts (just read the acknowledgments at the beginning of this book or the notes—bibliography—page at the end).

As good leaders, we understand that even though we most likely will take the brunt of this journey's beatings, especially since it is usually our passion we are working toward as an entrepreneur, we are not alone.

As leaders, we must understand that we are not alone. Even if we are solo artists or sole proprietors, and there is no one to call upon to help us do the work or grow the business, we are not truly alone. We must understand that even if we do not have a name to call upon or we don't see the results yet, help comes in many forms—financial, material, time, effort, encouragement, motivation, inspiration, hope. Good leaders know they got help somewhere along the journey, and they give proper credit, when possible, where credit is due. If we wish to be true leaders, we must show meekness when success is achieved and a level of power, or popularity, is garnered by setting our pride aside and acknowledging others.

A leader is honest.

As leaders, we must do our best to not tell lies, especially to ourselves.

Now, this one might be the trickiest to get right all the time because, every so often, we all have doubts and negativity that creep around in our mind and try to distort our thinking. Doubt and negativity then try to cover up our frailties with justifications and excuses for even the smallest of white lies. We all have weaknesses and quirks we may not always want to admit to ourselves; however, we must remember that if we are not fully honest with ourselves, then we cannot be fully honest with others in that same area, nor can we be fully honest about the potential issue or solution.

As leaders, we are responsible for the proper communication and understanding of the vision, and the best thing in communication is honesty. This honesty will be invaluable in reaching the proper solution and attaining our success.

Ben Goldacre has a great quote pertaining to science that I think also speaks just as well about being a leader. He says, "Science has authority, not because of white coats, or titles, but because of precision and transparency: you explain your theory, set out your evidence, and reference the studies that support your case."[3]

Okay. Now you might say, "Could you make like the cat hanging from the clothesline on those overused motivational pictures and hold on a second? How in the world does this equate to being a leader?"

That is another excellent question. This is also a good chance to demonstrate the importance of communication. So, let's rephrase that previous quote just a bit so you can better understand what I mean. (The bold text are my additions.)

> "**Leadership** has authority, not because of **position**, or titles, but because of **serving** and **honest communication**: you explain **the issue and possible ramifications (even if you somehow caused the issue)**, set out your **plan of correction**, and reference **your team to help** support your case."

Remember, even if you are a solo entrepreneur, you still have a team, those trusted people—friends, family, etc.—on whom you rely on for feedback and honesty. So, if you want them to be honest with you, then you need to be honest with them.

As leaders, we must understand that the saying "honesty will set you free" is true. We should understand that whether we are honest or not, we cannot escape the consequences of choices made, but by being honest, we can better the chances of finding a solution, salvaging relationships, and limiting and repairing any damage that might have occurred. Honesty will not eliminate consequences, but it will help set us free from complete and total collapse.

A leader does not accept excuses or allow justification from themselves.

To be good leaders, we must admit the truth to ourselves.

Once again, we see that honesty is very important.

Truth, the whole truth and nothing but the truth, is another hard aspect of leadership, entrepreneurship, and life. Why is that? Because we have believed something that is not true. We have accepted the idea that a half-truth is still the truth, but by omitting part of the truth, we have altered another's perception of the truth and, in doing so, we have planted an untruth (a lie) in that person's mind. The omission then changes our own view of the truth. No matter how much we, or anyone, try to change someone's perception of the truth, the truth will always remain the truth. It is the whole truth that is required for honesty to be fully present.

We must also put in the time required to study and research to find the truth, to find what it is we need to learn from a mistake or perceived failure, correct it, and then we can move on.

I have seen too many people, myself included, make excuse after excuse for a failure and justify our self-sabotaging ways to avoid the responsibility and acceptance of what was or could have been. In doing so, we negate the opportunities, learning, and growth that would and should come from such defeats.

To be true leaders, we need to hold our tongue and not blame others for our failures; we accept them, embrace them, learn from them, and, in doing so, we are able to find the opportunities to grow to levels that were previously unattainable.

A leader inspires.

As leaders, we are to inspire ourselves and others to continue the chosen journey. To inspire is to fulfill those desires and questions of how and why someone is making a difference with what they are doing. Why does the successful entrepreneur keep getting up every day and perform the hard work required to achieve his dream, even in the face of all the mental doubts and fears, the physical exhaustion, and the emotional stress of finances? How is he able to keep his dream alive, keep his hope up, keep the fire burning inside, even when his journey seems dark and stormy? Inspiration is the lighthouse that keeps shining to guide the entrepreneur to his success. Inspiration is how we keep ourselves moving when the darkness comes, and the wishing well seems dry and empty. Inspiration is an inside-out approach.

Fill yourself with good, positive, and uplifting Words, and you fill yourself with inspiration.

As leaders, we must understand that motivation is temporary and contingent upon outside forces (money, awards, bonuses, fame) and that those outside forces fade with each passing moment. To inspire is to ignite that flame deep inside, that passion and drive for a purpose greater than the temporary, greater than ourselves. It is the vision, the purpose, the reason for pushing through trials and tribulation, and it is what tells us to, in the words of former U.S. President Ronald Reagan, "[insert your name here], tear down this wall."[4] The wall of doubt, confusion, and fear stands no chance against inspiration. Inspiration is more than us and our material gains; it is how we can better another spirit, person, business, community, society, and nation.

Most importantly, a leader is a servant.

Jack Welch said it well: "Before you are a leader, success is all about growing yourself. When you become a leader, success is all about growing others."[5]

Of course, we must take care of ourselves. We discussed that in the prologue. But we must not forget about others along the way, and especially when we reach our success.

It is very difficult to lead a venture, a business, people, or a nation if one does not serve others.

When we serve others, we will also serve ourselves.

As the saying goes, "you reap what you sow." The question here is, do you want to reap a life and entrepreneurial journey of solitude, bitterness, and envy, or do you want to reap a life and entrepreneurial journey of friendship, blessing, and generosity?

Throughout life, we will all have the opportunity to serve, but, as leaders, that opportunity will come with more compound consequences for ourselves and possibly others.

As servants, we will serve our customers, we will serve our partners, we will serve our employees, we will serve our community, we will serve our mission statement, we will serve our business, we will serve our vision, and in return, we will serve ourselves.

As leaders, we must understand that we are leading toward a singular vision, a purpose that should, and most of us would hope, outlive even us. To do so, we must serve, and then we will be served by our vision in return.

In 1988, deep in the Motilandia jungles of northeastern Columbia, a missionary and entrepreneur in his own way, traveled down the river toward his destination where the Motilones Bari Indian tribe lived. The Motilones Bari were a primitive and very savage tribe. The brave journeyman, Bruce Olson, had visited this tribe many years before and was eventually welcomed by them. Throughout his years visiting this tribe, he managed to bring the message of God to them, as well as establishing medical clinics and schools for modern society's forgotten people in the jungles. Because of his work and generosity, he became known in Columbia, and he became a popular target of the Communist guerrilla revolutionaries who frequented Columbia with violence, terror, and selfish bloodshed, for territorial control and personal and political agendas.

Well, on this fateful trip down the river, he and his boatmates were unknowingly traveling directly toward a Communist guerrilla group waiting to ambush them. When Olson and his boatmates reached the dock, the guerillas were waiting, guns in hand, to take Olson captive by any means necessary. Olson, knowing the seriousness of the situation and that these men were only there for him, willingly walked toward his would-be kidnappers, willing to sacrifice himself in an attempt to save those who were travelling with him. Olson spent nine long, grueling, torturous months in captivity at the hands of these revolutionary, idealistic guerrilla fighters. These men spent much time physically torturing Olson in horrible ways, attempting to get him to speak for them and their agendas by joining their cause. They knew his name held political power, and they hoped they could break him so they might advance their agendas through him.

During his time in brutal captivity, he did not give in to anger, hate, selfishness, or a similar form of evil brutality that his kidnappers reveled in each day. He did not go 80's Hollywood macho man, ripping his shirt off, speaking one-liner action quips, breaking necks, blowing up guerilla outposts with guns blazing, all while flexing his biceps and saving the girl (there was no girl). Quite the opposite. He chose a path that most of us probably would not even have thought about. He chose to be humble; he chose to teach them. Most of these guerilla fighters were illiterate. Olsen, not under force or conversion, decided to show peace and love by teaching them how to read and write in their native language. He was held captive for the duration it took to teach them to read and write well enough—it was a nine-month captivity. Olson, not because he turned traitor or because his kidnappers received any form of payment for their hostage, was released by these same Communist guerilla revolutionary men who had first desired to either kill, convert, or trade him for political power and gain.

Olson, through his actions when first captured, showed true leadership in his understanding of "the buck stops here." He knew these people were after him, and by willingly giving himself up, he could protect his boatmates and spare the lives of others.

He showed leadership by teaching and mentoring his kidnappers through the education of reading and writing.

He showed leadership by not accepting any excuse or justification for his situation, such as by sulking in the thoughts of blaming others for his choice to continue to do good works in a dangerous and violent Columbia.

He was honest with his intentions to show love and mercy when these men deserved neither.

He chose to serve (in a non-threatening way that could hopefully, one day, bring about an opportunity for peaceful negotiations and end the bloodshed), and by serving others, he was served himself; he was released from captivity.[6]

HARD WORK

"There is no substitute for hard work."[1]

– Thomas A. Edison

An Entrepreneur must be:

A HARD WORKER

Entrepreneurship is a hard and difficult task, which will take great risk and much commitment, but it also comes with the potential for even greater rewards.

Starting a business, be it brick and mortar, online, or as a freelancer, or even stepping out to chase our dream, our passion, is not all fun and games. It takes many, many, many hours of hard work to make it a reality.

To be a hard worker, we must be willing to get in the trenches, get dirty, get beaten up, take the hits, and do the work ourselves as needed; and rest assured, it will be needed, there is no question or doubt about that. If we decide to be entrepreneurs, then we will need to spend long hours researching and reading materials on our chosen field, learn the market, attend those events to make those contacts and make those sales calls, sacrifice time with family and friends and time doing those extracurricular activities we enjoy, sacrifice personal finances to help build and support our growing venture, and put in long days and nights to get the client their product and service, because, in the beginning at least, we most likely will be the only ones to call on when hard work is required; for we are the entrepreneurs.

As Dave Ramsey says, "The most important decision about your goals is not what you're willing to do to achieve them, but what you are willing to give up."[2]

When it comes to hard work and asking the question, "What am I willing to give up to achieve my dream?" I can definitely say, "Been there, done that."

I remember that many, many, many times as I worked on videos for a small media company my friend, Ryan, and I ran together years ago called Two Titans Media L.L.C., I would work long hours, sometimes late into the night, which caused me to miss meals with my family, just to ensure the videos we were hired to create were completed on time and above expectations for the client. I remember practically living in coffee shops; we would spend countless hours, months even, working on our business plan, website, contracts, budget, and all those necessary components for a business to survive. It was mind-numbing work researching aspects of business in which we did not have much knowledge or any enjoyment doing, just so we could spend about ten-percent of our time doing aspects of business we did enjoy—the creative process of writing, video, and photography.

We would research, write, rewrite, make mistakes, research some more, rewrite again, and then realize that we were wrong and made even more mistakes once again. Then we would research again, rewrite again, and then, finally, after many tries and failures, we would achieve success in our goals with our website, business offerings, prices, contracts, and marketing. Then, after some time, we would once again realize even more hard work would be required to correct yet another mistake we made, which led to another failure. It was the hard work and willingness to learn from and correct mistakes and failures that allowed us to grow and endure for as long as we did.

Even though, at the time of writing this book, the business is on temporary hiatus, the entrepreneurial journey we took together strengthened our friendship, taught us valuable life lessons and gave us the knowledge (in some cases the knowledge of what not to do) to be able to help others on their entrepreneurial journey. If it were not for those experiences with that entrepreneurial business venture, we might not have met Rick—the gentleman mentioned in the acknowledgments with whom we helped produce a podcast show, for which I was one of the producers, creative designers, and audio engineers. If we had never met him, we would not have had the opportunity to help create an inspirational and educational podcast to inform people of history and give them inspiration through personal and historical stories so they could make positive choices and push through troubled times in their life.[3]

In other words, the hard work required during our entrepreneurial venture with our media company, Two Titans Media, together with years of sustained effort to help others build their ideas of success, according to their personal goals, and assiduously stepping out to undertake other entrepreneurial ventures, led us to understand that we, just like anyone else, look to others for help and inspiration during the storms of life. And as mentioned in chapter two, it is the end story that we endured and how we survived those times of need that help others. So, even though there were hard and extremely difficult and trying times, and that particular podcast has since been discontinued, in the end, it was all worth it for us.

However, it is very important to understand that hard work must be combined with a focus on the vision, the purpose, and the goal to be achieved. Without this focus, we greatly increase our chances of diverting our attention and effort into areas that do not lead us to our goal, to reaching our vision, and to accomplishing our purpose. If we do not have focus, then all our hard work will, most likely, result in a lack of direction, which could cause chaos, stress, exhaustion, and depression from a lack of perceived accomplishment.

Hard work is a key characteristic of a successful entrepreneur and any person who reaches their success.

As entrepreneurs, we must be willing to put in the hard work.

As I mentioned earlier, in the beginning, at least, we most likely will be the only ones to call on when hard work is required.

It was early in the year when two gentlemen received a knock at the door. No, it was not Dave[4]; it was opportunity. It was not just any opportunity, but the elusive opportunity to achieve a goal they had been working toward, without success, for a long time. This opportunity, however, came with a string attached, a string they would later learn was invaluable to achieving success; a string some people are hanging on to by a thread (pun intended): They would need to be servants to another. As long as they worked hard to help each other, and this other person, achieve their goal, these two gentlemen increased their chances of achieving theirs. By serving another, they would themselves be served.

"Finally," they thought, "we can achieve this elusive dream of creating a great short film that is not a student film, or a film that consists of just the two of us as the cast or, more specifically, the only crew."

They were overly excited about this opportunity.

This opportunity came with even more great news. They were informed that the script had already been written (completed), the film had already been cast (the actors were already selected), the shot list (a checklist of the camera shots desired to edit a scene together) had already been prepared, some locations had already been secured, a cinematographer (camera operator) had already signed to be on board, and that a few other people had already expressed interest in helping as crew. The icing on the cake was that this film could be created on a low-budget—low budget for these two gentlemen meant anything between zero dollars and five-hundred dollars—and the end product would still look fantastic with the equipment they had in their possession, which was minimal.

They looked at each other and said, "This is going to be great! A walk in the park. No hard work at all."

This opportunity knocking at their door was almost too good to be true.

In unison they said, "What could possibly go wrong?"

With that one question, these two dreamers began their long and arduous journey toward being recognized filmmakers in their community.

Throughout their journey, making this film and chasing one of their dreams, they encountered much difficulties and a myriad of perceived failures that should have, and at times almost did, set them so far back on their journey that the light at the end of their entrepreneurial tunnel seemed so small and distant that it was almost non-existent.

First, even before filming, they encountered problems with the script when it came to the discussed vision that the original creator expressed; problems that required many rewrites and, much to their frustration, rewrites the day before a few scenes were scheduled to be filmed. Every time they assumed every issue was fixed and every hurdle was leaped successfully (well, successfully to them, because things were still hobbling forward), another problem would raise its head to say, "Hello, I work for Murphy, and his law must be upheld."

Scheduling issues, equipment failures, human errors in production requiring reshoots, major inclement weather mysteriously occurring exactly on the scheduled production days (what do you expect in Oklahoma?), commitment issues, and the opportunity to prove the adage of what happens when one attempts to assume: make an "ass" out of "u" and "me." An assumed to be simple and easy workload and already prepared short film that should have taken maybe a few weeks to complete ended up taking them on a detour that would reward them with many valuable life lessons and numerous opportunities to grow.

This part of their entrepreneurial journey for growth took four long years of much, as stated in a previous chapter, hard work, commitment, determination, hard work, persistence, perseverance, hard work, positivity, creativity, and hard work, that left them, in the end, practically as the only crew yet again for both the production and post-production of the film. They were so beaten down by failures and negativity from others, and sometimes even from their own thinking and mouth, that every time the light at the end of the tunnel grew big enough to bring hope to their beaten souls, it came accompanied with the thundering sound of a locomotive rumbling along at full speed and then, just like a penny placed on the railroad tracks, they were once again flattened and bent by another problem that ran them over.

However, through their hard work and the hard work of a few who occasionally came to help and motivate them and help keep them inspired throughout the filmmaking process, they were able to achieve their dream. The other person witnessed their goal, their version of success, of their story coming to life on the big screen at a film festival. These two gentlemen witnessed their goal, their version of success; as the film went on to win an award for Best Picture Oklahoma Soil Short Film at that same festival.

Through commitment and a considerable amount of focused hard work, these two gentlemen were able to help in the service of providing success for another, and, in turn, they were rewarded with their own success.

5

DECISION MAKER

"Waiting hurts. Forgetting hurts. But not knowing which decision to take can sometimes be the most painful..."[1]
– José N. Harris

An Entrepreneur must be:

A DECISION MAKER

As entrepreneurs, we are required to make numerous decisions each and every day, both in our personal life and in our business life. In fact, everyone is required to make numerous decisions each and every day; whether we accept that responsibility or blame shift, it is still our decision. But as entrepreneurs, we are not always afforded the opportunity to be able to wait for someone else to decide for us. Too many people wait for someone else to make a decision for them and to tell them what needs to be done. Too many people sit back, dreaming about a desired outcome, but do nothing because a decision is required that will demand sacrifice, responsibility, and accountability—this decision is most likely accompanied by its good friend, but our trepidation, risk. Do not get me wrong here, this is not necessarily a bad thing, seeing as these people can be, and most times are, hard workers with great skill in what they do; they just appear to be unable to make the quick or difficult decision, and/or unwilling to accept the responsibility and accountability of the decision.

As entrepreneurs, we must be willing to make difficult decisions in a quick and timely manner with the knowledge and understanding we have at that moment. Of course, this will be easier to accomplish if we understand the vision and have put in the time and done the hard work to research and plan as much as possible before the question is even raised and the answer is required.

When it comes to decision making, especially for small things, I know I personally like to try and make a decision as quickly as possible, and then I tell myself, "The decision was made. Deal with it and move on." Of course, I, like everyone else, am human, and sometimes that risk, that fear, does win in delaying my decision making; we are all in the same boat with this human behavior sometimes, though we must learn to overcome it as much as possible. There is, however, one area where I believe a quick decision could possibly be detrimental and unfavorable to the individual, and that is when a contract is involved.

I find it best for myself, and I think it is best for everyone, to take the time to read the contract and ensure it says what we want, or, at the very least, see what we can come to a compromise on if we do not like a requirement or an aspect of it, before signing. Even then, though, a decision must be made in a timely manner with a degree of certainty and a level of confidence.

Now, each of us are, in some form or fashion in our daily lives, a decision maker. It is the level (small or big, individual or global) of the decision required and the possible consequences of the decision (inconvenient or life and death) that set the true decision maker apart from others—it sets the entrepreneur apart from others.

There are two important aspects of decision making—one is the ability to make the difficult, big, and sometimes costly decisions; and the second is the ability to make the small and seemingly inconsequential decisions, and to make those decisions fast. Being a decision maker is something that each of us must learn and improve on throughout our lives.

As entrepreneurs, we cannot always afford to be wishy-washy, waffling, or flip-flop. We will find ourselves in situations that require a decision to be made fast, without much preparation, and without hesitation. A quick, firm, decisive, and confident answer will sometimes be the difference between opening the door when opportunity knocks or missing its visit and wrestling with doubt, the "what if" of regret.

All right then, how do we improve on our decision making skills?

Decision coach Nell Wulfhart briefly explains how to train oneself to be able to make decisions and make them quickly, "If you're chronically indecisive, build that decision-making muscle by starting small. Give yourself 30 seconds to decide what you'll have for dinner, what movie to watch, or whether you want to go out tonight. Follow through on that decision. Repeat. Then work up to bigger things... Making small decisions in a timely fashion will help train your brain to think through questions more quickly."[2]

However, as with all decisions, there will be a cause and effect. This is where the rub of decision making comes into play. We must remember that not every decision we make will please people or be viewed as great, nor will each decision we make even take us in the proper direction to reach our goals; but each one is important and must be made in a timely manner with a degree of certainty and a level of confidence.

Decision making is not a matter of choosing what might seem like the best answer just so we, hopefully, do not offend anyone. We cannot please all the people all the time. It is about making the decision we believe would be best for us, best for the vision, best for reaching the goal, and, hopefully, doing so without compromising our values, ethics, morals, or deep beliefs. It is about making the decision so we do not fracture our foundation and allow the seeds of corruption to implant themselves through peer-pressure or lack of roots, and this comes from being grounded on a firm foundation. Another way to look at decision making is that it is not about trying not to offend anyone because, as mentioned earlier, we cannot please everyone, but, rather, who we are comfortable offending. Being a decision maker is tough and sometimes unpleasant. Some decisions will turn out to be mistakes that could lead us to a perceived failure but, if we act as leaders should, we will accept the responsibility of these decisions, be honest about the mistake, learn from any perceived failure, turn it into a positive opportunity to learn, and hopefully grow.

There will always be people who celebrate with us and think we made the right decision, just as there will always be people who jeer us and think we made the wrong decision. As a decision maker, we will be a hero to some and a villain to others. It will not always be easy, but a leader's job—an entrepreneur's job—is not an easy one.

It was early in the evening on a hot and sunny summer day. The children of the neighborhood, bored with the restrictive rules to stay indoors when the summer heat peaked past triple digits (because of their parents' fear of sunburns and heat-stroke), were overjoyed by the sudden drop in temperature that allowed them to finally play outside. The children, with the energy of a young puppy after eating a bag full of coffee beans, ran to their favorite spot to play.

They arrived at their favorite play place, a place they knew very well: the railroad tracks. The children immediately began to play "hot lava"—the game where you pretend the ground is hot lava and you must not step on it, otherwise you burn alive. They used the railroad tracks and railroad ties as their solid base to avoid being burned alive.

There were two sets of railroad tracks at this location that were separated by no more than fifteen feet of a flat, messy, dirt median covered with some rocks. A dozen kids were playing on the tracks that day. Eleven of them were playing on the railroad tracks located on the South side of the rocky, dirt median, and one child was playing on the North side tracks. The North side tracks were closed; they had been out of use for nearly two years, and the earth was already beginning to reclaim a part of the land they were built on. Small patches of grass and a few weeds were protruding from between the rocks, wrapping around the tracks and breaking up part of the ground. The South side tracks, however, were still in use by the railways, and a train traversed those tracks nearly every day. About a half mile East from where the kids were playing, there was a railroad switch for the tracks. Though the switch was slightly rusting from lack of use, it still functioned as it was built to do.

A person, who decided to take a shortcut home from work that day, just happened to be walking by the railroad switch when a train was approaching. This person, hearing the train, turned East and saw the train no more than one hundred yards from where they now stood, and they could begin to feel the rumbling vibrations of the train traveling through the ground and vibrating their feet. The train was approaching fast. This person turned the other direction and saw the kids playing on the railroad tracks. Immediately, this person began waving their arms and shouting at the top of their lungs for the kids to move.

"Hey!" this person shouted, "You kids, get off the tracks! There is a train coming! Get off the tracks!"

The kids were too far away to hear this person shouting at them and, even if they were not, they were having too much fun and were too involved in their hot lava game to notice that someone was attempting to warn them of the approaching train. The children were completely oblivious of the imminent danger.

This person looked again at the oncoming train and realized there was no way to warn the kids in time; it was only fifty yards away now. This person looked at the railroad switch and decided this switch was the only option left to save any of the kids. The train was approaching very fast, and there were only seconds before it reached the switch, the point of no return. With the last remaining seconds, this person's heart pounded at what felt like the same rate of the rumbling train—palms were sweating, breathing was intense and came in short inhales and exhales, the mind raced, and the legs trembled as this person grabbed the switch and tried to mentally race through the options.

If I pull the switch, this person thought, *then the train would change tracks, and its new course would be on the North tracks where the one kid who chose to play safely on the closed railroad tracks would surely be killed. That is, if the tracks were not too decayed from not being used or maintained for two years, in which case the train could derail and potentially kill anyone on board.* This person looked toward the kids and thought, *However, if I do not pull the switch, then the train would continue on its current path and kill all eleven children playing on the South side tracks—the tracks everyone knew were unsafe to be on.*

"What should I do?!" this person shouted.

Should the kids who chose to ignore the rules and warnings and play where it was unsafe (where the tracks were still in use and where a train could come and possibly injure or kill them) be sacrificed?

Should the one kid who chose to obey the rules, listen to the warnings, and play where it was safe to play, who now stood on the tracks that were closed, be sacrificed?

Should the lives of those on the train be considered along with the lone child if the switch was pulled?[3]

There are only mere seconds to decide.

Who should live and who should die?

You are this person.

You have found yourself in a situation that requires a decision to be made fast and without much preparation and without hesitation.

What do you do?

RISK-TAKER

"If you risk nothing, then you risk everything."[1]

– Geena Davis

An Entrepreneur must be:

A RISK-TAKER

R isk is an inevitable part of life and success.

As entrepreneurs, we must be willing to take risks, both big and small. If we are unwilling to accept risk, then how will we ever be able to step out and try new things, learn new skills, or even expect to grow in any capacity?

Taking a risk means putting faith in the unknown; it is having hope in the unseen for positive results; it is about believing in our future by investing precious time and valuable resources into the journey, and doing so with an opportunistic mindset. As it states in Hebrews 11:1, "Now faith is confidence in what we hope for and assurance about what we do not see."[2] It is a combination of personal choices and the consequences of those choices.

When I say "risk," I am not talking about running to the nearest casino and risking your life savings on the toss of the dice. Or as Kipling said in his poem *IF*, "risk it on one turn of pitch-and-toss."[3] What I am talking about is a calculated risk; that is the weighing of the pros and cons, or advantages and disadvantages, of a decision or venture. It is the estimated amount of loss or gain you might be exposed to after the risk is undertaken. In other words, a calculated risk is the risk taken after some research and deliberation has been done—this is where those long, sacrificial hours of research and hard work mentioned previously really come into play.

Risk-taking will be rewarding if we can progress toward our goal or, at the very least, choose to learn from it, but it may not always lead us to success. Yet, without risk, we are almost guaranteed no success.

However, risk-taking will inevitably lead us to opportunity, and opportunity allows us a chance to learn, grow, and potentially reach our success.

I never thought of myself as a great or professional writer (even though God did), so when I began writing this information many years ago, I was not sure if I could finish writing this material, or if the information would be intelligibly communicated through my writing. However, I stepped out and invested many hours—years, in fact—slowly working on this book, and finding and garnering much resources and experience on this entrepreneurial journey where I gathered much of this information. In other words, I took a big risk stepping out on this journey, gathering this information, writing this book and, especially, publishing and releasing this book for you, the reader, to potentially be a critic. (Although I believe you are enjoying this book and are able to use this information to better your life and the life of others.) If I did not take the risk, I would never have encountered the numerous opportunities that have helped me gain the knowledge I have today, nor would this book be in existence. In fact, the journey taken to get this book finished and to print it began as a short blog; it was then rewritten as a short podcast script (but was never recorded), and then, eventually, it was expanded and became this very book. The risk I took appeared to fail at first, but because the risk was taken, my endeavor grew and grew; through perceived failure from the initial risk, you now have the printed success in your hands. Who knew? God knew!

Remember, nothing in life is guaranteed, but most everything in life can be attainable with some degree of risk.

Risk-taking is not always about the final outcome of success or failure, but about the willingness to step out of our ordinary and invest a part of ourselves in the potential. Without being willing to take a risk, we will not be able to face success or failure.

The soil was damp from a fresh rainstorm that hydrated the earth, and a cool wind blew as the trees swayed back and forth, revealing a beat of their own. The leaves of the trees dripped with the purity of mother nature's refreshing nutrients. On the edge of one of the tree's branches hung three acorns, rocking back and forth with the wind while in deep discussion with one another.

"I am going to break away from this branch and leave my current place among this tree behind," said The First Acorn.

"I'm worried about what might happen if we let go," replied The Second Acorn.

The First Acorn responded, "If we stay, then this is all there ever will be for us, and our life will be short. We are acorns, and we cannot reach our full potential, or survive for long, just hanging here."

"Maybe," answered The Third Acorn, "but at least we know what we have here. You can risk it all if you wish. As for me, I will spend what little time I have staying right here. It may not be all I was created for, but it is safe enough, for now. Besides, it is better to be safe than sorry."

With that, The First Acorn said, "Fare well," and he let go and fell to the ground.

A few seconds later, The Second Acorn decided to take a risk and follow The First Acorn, and he, too, let go and fell to the ground.

Entrepreneur

Once they were on the ground, they noticed small creatures running about, gathering other acorns and items in their mouths and then scurrying off. One of the small creatures then ran up the tree they had just fallen from and snatched up their friend, who decided to remain.

"If we don't want to be taken like him, then we better bury ourselves fast," said The First Acorn.

Quickly, the two acorns twisted and wiggled their way into the soft and damp soil. They dug themselves down so far that they no longer could see the small creatures or even the faintest of light.

"It's dark down here," said The Second Acorn.

"Yes, it is," replied The First Acorn, "but it is safe, for now."

The Second Acorn asked, with a sense of worry in his voice, "This was your idea, so what do we do now?"

The First Acorn responded, "Now, we grow."

Confused and scared, The Second Acorn said, "Grow? You mean go back up there with those creatures! We will get eaten."

"Maybe," said The First Acorn.

The Second Acorn argued, "Our lives could be shorter than the life of our friend who stayed hanging on to the tree."

The First Acorn said, "Our lives have already surpassed the life of our friend, and we have been somewhere and learned new knowledge that he never did." Then, he reiterated, "We grow." He continued, saying, "I want to stretch my roots and dig deeper into the soil. I want to work hard and develop the habit of roots so that I might have a chance to survive whatever we might encounter up there. I want to take a risk and exit this dark yet comfortable and complacent lifestyle. I want to stand tall and reach the sky."

"Why?" asked The Second Acorn. "Why risk what we have here and now? Why risk safety? Why risk security? Why risk losing our small, confined, enriched, hidden, and safe spot?"

There was a moment of silence.

Then, The First Acorn asked, "Why would you want to stay hidden? Why would you want to keep your dreams, your gifts, and your life, buried in the dark, beneath the soil?"

The Second Acorn hesitantly said, "I am afraid. I know what I have here, deep within the soil. I do not know what is up there, waiting for me. What if I spread my roots deep within the soil and find danger waiting just below? What if I break through the ground? I would be exposed to the world! What if the world up there does not like me? What if I reveal myself, and I am not accepted? What if when I reveal myself and try to grow, I get taken by those creatures before I can grow tall enough to survive?"

"What if they don't? What if we do break free, and what if we grow so big, so tall, that all those creatures look up to us? What if our risk pays off, and we can once again feel the cool breeze of a beautiful spring day, feel the warmth of the sun and its nourishing rays, and sway and dance in the rain? What if our risk, our struggle, pays off, and we become the next tree that provides life and opportunity for the next acorn? Isn't that a risk worth taking?" replied The First Acorn.

As time passed, The First Acorn grew. His roots traveled deep in the ground and held him firm; his trunk grew wide and thick and tall; his branches extended far and wide, providing shelter for smaller creatures, and giving life to future potential acorn trees. His risks were rewarded with opportunity for further growth, and his growth took him to heights beyond his imagination. He was now living his dream.

The Second Acorn remained below the surface, holding onto his current perceived safety. He chose not to take further risk, fearing the unknown, and fearing the loss of what little he currently had. He never again saw the light of day, felt the warmth of the sun, enjoyed the cool breeze of spring, or grew. He, along with his dreams, talents, hopes, and future, remained buried deep beneath the earth, in the dark, until he rotted and died.

Will you be like The Third Acorn and remain stationary, never taking that first step, never taking a risk to let go, to grow, to learn, and to achieve your dream?

Will you be like The Second Acorn and risk only so much as to find a more comfortable place to hide, never fully tempting failure, too afraid to let the world see you, too afraid to face potential criticism, and leave your dreams, your skills, and your potential success buried six feet under?

Will you be like The First Acorn and take a risk to allow your skills to shine and your dreams to grow and become reality?

Will you take a risk and allow the opportunity for your success to be obtained?

7

SUCCEED & FAIL

"Success is getting what you want. Happiness is wanting what you get."[1] – Dale Carnegie

An Entrepreneur must be:

WILLING TO SUCCEED AND WILLING TO FAIL

Too many people avoid taking the lead, taking a risk, making tough decisions, and they avoid their dreams for one reason or another. Most of these reasons, however, are based on fear.

And fear is the number one killer of hopes and dreams.

As Les Brown states, "The graveyard is the richest place on earth, because it is here that you will find all the hopes and dreams that were never fulfilled, the books that were never written, the songs that were never sung, the inventions that were never shared, the cures that were never discovered, all because someone was too afraid to take that first step, keep with the problem, or determined to carry out their dream."[2]

"I would do XYZ if only I knew where to start or how to find the right sources to know how to begin."

So, because we do not know where or how to properly begin, we justify burying our dream with a false rationalization of ignorance, all because we are too afraid to take that first step. Because we do not know the solution to the problem, or exactly where to look for the answer, we are too afraid to put in the hard work to find the solution. Because we do not want to take any chance of losing what material items or political gain or title to our name that we might have at this moment, we are too afraid to take the risk of achieving our dream. Because we are too afraid to take on more responsibility or accept any accountability for a potential wrong decision, which could lead to a perceived failure, we are too afraid to take the risk of achieving our dream, reaching a goal, and obtaining our success.

Creativity, one of the qualities mentioned in chapter two, in between the many instances of hard work, is essential for dream chasing. Without creativity, one would never know how to begin, how to fix a mistake, how to expand on an idea, how to improve, or how to keep pushing forward in the face of failure. Creativity is not just for artists and entertainers; creativity is inside everyone. It is our imagination. It is how we create a positive from a negative and reach our success. Creativity is the quality of being creative and the ability to, well, create.[3]

Thomas Edison is known as the "Father of Invention," however, he, too, had to be creative, work hard, take risks, and be willing to fail so he might finally succeed. As Edison once said, "I have not failed 10,000 times—I have successfully found 10,000 ways that will not work." One of his failed inventions was an electronic vote recorder that he was sure would save countless hours by automatically tallying the votes of officials voting on bills. To his dismay, the machine was quickly dismissed and forgotten—an epic failure for the man who was so confident that this one invention would set him for life. How crushing and defeating that must have felt! Edison, however, did not let this failure stop him, nor did he let any future fear of rejection or failure get in his way. What did he do? He worked hard and decided to focus his efforts and creativity on a singular vision, "He vowed he would not invent a technology that didn't have an apparent market; that he wasn't going to invent things for the sake of inventing them… but to be able to sell them."[4]

Edison used his creativity to invent contraptions that were not even in existence in most people's nightly dreams. He used his creativity to figure out ways around a mistake, or failure, to improve on items and technology already in existence, to press onward toward success. He failed repeatedly, and yet, because of his hard work and commitment to his entrepreneurial dream, his persistence and perseverance through his crushing defeats and failures, and his positivity and creativity in the face of fear to find a new starting point and keep pushing forward, he is revered in history for his successful inventions.

Fear, as I have heard repeated many times before, is an acronym for 'False Evidence Appearing Real.' Fear rarely has anything to do with the current reality, but everything to do with hijacking our creativity. Fear warps our creativity to the negative and worrisome. Fear is usually of the unknown. It is the "what if" of negative thinking and doubt. When we face our fear, whether it be of failure or of success, we have one of two choices: we can either 'Face Everything And Rise' or we can 'Forget Everything And Run.' If we face our fear, we must also accept the fact that any possible failure is a learning experience, a stepping stone to our ultimate success. If we run from our fear, we have then chosen to bury our dream, bury our entrepreneurial journey in "one of the richest places on earth."[5]

Our fear of failure tells us lies such as: "If I don't try, then I can't fail." That in and of itself is a form of failure; remember, failure is only permanent if one stops trying, and when one stops trying, that will almost certainly bring about a lack of what one would perceive as success. If we do not try, we will not succeed.

Failure is nothing more than the real world's classroom. Everyone must be a student and attend this class at some point in their life—There is no skipping this class. It is mandatory, and it will find each of us and teach us its lessons. Believe me, you will encounter perceived failure. But it is not the class (failure) that determines our future; it is what we choose to do with the classroom teaching that does.

So, all of us must ask ourselves these important questions about the subject of failure.

Will I sleep through class and be a repeat student, forever formulating excuses and justifications for why someone else, external circumstances, or the world, are causing me to repeat the grade? In other words, will I always point the finger?

"It's not my fault!"

Will I pack my bags and go home, convinced that the class is too hard, too life-shattering, too hurtful and oppressive toward my feelings, ego, skill, or intellect?

"Life's too hard. I just can't do it."

Will I arrive to class with a desire for learning, an optimistic attitude toward the lesson, and an opportunistic vision toward the result?

"I have taken a rocky path and have had many bricks dropped on me, but I will use those bricks to build a strong foundation, and upon that foundation, I shall place those rocks as the steps I need to reach my success."

The Walt Disney Company understands that failure is a part of life, and they even embrace it and encourage their employees in taking the risk of it. By now, most people have probably heard that Walt Disney had many failures, from bankruptcy to losing control of one of his creations, to being terminated from a job for his supposed lack of creativity. Yet, he kept trying and facing failure head-on. Through the risk of failure, Walt Disney was able to create a legacy.

According to Michael Eisner, Disney holds a meeting a few times a year in which they encourage their employees to pitch any idea they have for a full-length animated feature film (no matter how ridiculous, outrageous, or bad the idea might sound) to top-level executives. The meeting is done in a similar manner to the old television game show, "*The Gong Show*," of the 1970s. If for any reason an executive does not like the pitch, they bang the gong, and the pitch is over. He says that this fun and engaging idea has encouraged their employees to pitch their ideas, and, in doing so, they feel valued for having been listened to, and they also have a chance to see their creativity and their idea of success brought to life on the big screen. He further stated that this is how certain films such as *Hercules* came to be.[6] By embracing their fear of failure, they were able to turn it into a positive outcome.

We must also remember, though, that failure can also come in the form of self-sabotage—a fear of success.

Fear of success can also be a fear of change. We, as humans, can have a tendency to become complacent with where we are in life and what we do. We can come to a place where we understand what is required of us and expected of us; we then become complacent and stagnant in our lives. We might even begin to think, "Better safe than sorry." In this state, we might fear that success will change how others perceive us and who we are. The truth is, we are either getting better or worse, but we are rarely just maintaining. With leading, taking risks, and a willingness to tempt failure and achieve our success, we leave our security blanket of our comfort zone and attempt to no longer, as the saying might go, "fly under the radar."

We understand that with success comes change, and this fear of change can cause us to fail ourselves. For, "If I don't succeed, then people won't expect more from me, and I will not have to deal with possible future failures or embarrassments."

We must not be afraid of failure or success, for, in each of those, we are promised the ability to reach for and achieve something far greater than what we currently have in our grasp. Without taking the lead, working hard, taking a risk, and tempting failure, we would not have (or have received) the gifts, the lessons, or the opportunities that help us to grow and reach our success—these are truly blessings in our lives.

As Bruce Wilkinson states in his book *The Dream Giver*, "You can either feel comfort and give up your Dream, or you can feel fear and pursue your Dream."[7]

To conquer failure and reach our success, we must be willing to take a risk by making the decision to work hard and lead through serving others.

Then, we can be entrepreneurs.

It had been days since Private Cole had stepped foot outside his hiding spot. He had been cowering in a dark and damp cellar of a house with a vineyard since his squad was ambushed nearly three days ago.

Private Cole was not born a coward; on the contrary, he used to play football in high school. Despite his small stature and lack of bulky muscles, he was a formidable defensive tackle, willing to sacrifice his own body for the game. Many times, he would face off against an opponent twice his size, in both height and muscle, and he refused to back down. Cole would stare them in the face as if looking deep into their soul until he found even the tiniest ounce of doubt, then he would turn that doubt into fear, shake their foundation with it, and take them off their game, just enough for him to gain the advantage. He was quick and cunning, a formidable combination when one lacks size. But now, he not only felt weak but sluggish and clouded with fear, stress, and regret; he was wallowing in his perceived failure.

His squad was ordered to mount a rescue mission for the owner of the vineyard and his family. The vineyard owner had risked everything to aid the Allies in their fight against the ruthless and evil Axis. He had gathered valuable intel, gave refuge to Allied soldiers and spies, helped the persecuted escape, and sabotaged enemy vehicles that stopped to rest on his property. He risked so much for the Allies, and now he was captured, probably being beaten and tortured, and completely relying on them to risk their lives, to risk failure to succeed in freeing him and his family from certain death. And yet, there no longer was a them; there was only him—the scared, fear-filled, and cowering man, hiding in these heroes' cellar. All was now resting upon the shoulders of Private Cole. The vineyard owner and his family, his squad mates, his own life, all rested in what he would do next.

"It's not my fault," Cole whispered to himself as he rocked back and forth. "I didn't know it was an ambush; none of us did."

He thought about the moment they began walking across the field. His squad Sergeant was in the lead, cautiously moving forward while scanning the building and landscape in front. To his Sergeant's left, and a few yards behind, was Harry, a tall thin man with a balding scalp that was revealed as he briefly removed his helmet to wipe the sweat dripping from his head. Just behind him was Lloyd, who was short but muscular and as tough as a rhino; in fact, Lloyd was the state champion in wrestling before he joined the military to serve his country and help in the fight to make evil tap-out and end this war. To the Sergeant's right, and a few yards behind, was Mike, a man of average height but with an athletic frame. He loved to play with explosives, which was probably why they made him the grenadier. Just behind him was Quinton, who stood over six feet tall and looked as if he could be the entire defensive line for Cole's high school football team; he was strong and resembled the epitome of the phrase "big boned," at least, that is what Quinton always said when asked about his weight. Bringing up the rear was Private Cole.

Private Cole remembered falling behind the group as they entered the field because Cole was their pack mule. He was the newest recruit, and, as such, he was to prove his worth and carry all the heavy gear—this was why he fell slightly behind. As he was approaching the tree line of the field, the enemy emerged from the house and surrounded his squad. Outnumbered and outgunned, they had no choice but to surrender. However, Cole had not yet been spotted. He dropped to the ground and hid where he was, watching his mates surrender their weapons and be marched off.

Private Cole shook his head, trying to erase this memory of his cowardice as he thought, *I should have been there with them. We should all be together now.*

A tear escaped his eyes and ran down his cheek.

"It's too hard. I can't do this on my own. I just can't do it," he said with a whimpered voice.

He remembered the faces his squad mates made as they were marched off—the disgust, fear, sadness, anger. Private Cole slapped himself in an attempt to beat these images out of his mind.

How could I be so selfish, so cowardly, so weak? he thought.

"I failed. I failed everyone. I failed myself. I am a failure," he said.

Cole began to get louder as he berated himself with regret and disgust for his actions.

"I am a failure. A worthless failure!" he shouted.

He kicked at a shelf next to him and, in his emotional state, hit it so hard that the whole thing fell over with a loud crash, as wood connected with concrete and glass wine bottles scattered all around. He jumped at the loud sound it made, immediately regretting his actions. He froze, listening for any noise, which might indicate that he had just failed again by revealing his hiding spot—this new home, which he made from his fearful and negative mindset in this dark and damp cellar, where he was sure he would also parish.

Cole's head jerked when he heard footsteps. It was the sound of quick, shuffling feet scurrying all around him, like a rat lost in a maze running back and forth, desperately trying to find the cheese it could smell was there, somewhere. The steps grew louder as they made their way closer to his dark corner of the world. He froze with fright as the footsteps approached and then, suddenly, stopped just ahead of him, somewhere in the shadows.

"Who's there?" asked Cole as the words barely wheezed their way out of his mouth.

There was a long moment of silence before a small bare foot stepped into the light, then the other. As Cole adjusted his eyes, he saw, standing before him, a small child, ragged, dirty, tired, and red-eyed from long periods of crying. Cole looked upon this child, this lost and lonely little girl, with a mixture of bewilderment and sadness.

Why was a child here, apparently alone?

And how long had this child been watching him?

"Where're your parents?" asked Cole.

She just stood there staring at him with questioning eyes.

Cole asked, "Are you alone? What's your name?"

Again, she did not answer. She just reached her arm out and extended an envelope toward Cole. He reluctantly took the envelope and slowly opened it, all while keeping one eye on the child and scanning the shadows with his other eye.

In the envelope, Cole found a letter. It appeared to be hastily written. It read:

To my Allied friends.

I hope my little girl stays safe long enough for you to receive this letter. I don't know how but my secret has been discovered. A trusted friend informed me that the Axis has learned that I have been helping you and attempting to save the lives of "scum"; their term, not mine. I only have a few minutes before they arrive. There is no time for my family or me to flee. We will be taken prisoner, and I fear we might never see the sunlight again. If you safely make it here, please take care of my child. I also wish to inform you where, I am confident, we will be taken. It is an unknown prison to most, well secreted from the world. It is a place I recently discovered and where traitors and Allied prisoners are taken when found in this region. It is marked on the attached map, along with what I believe are its weak points. I pray this letter finds its way into the right hands.

Private Cole dropped his hands to his lap as he looked up at the child. She was crying and shaking.

At that moment, Cole found his reserve. He had been emotionally defeated by his perceived failure and lack of self-worth and mentally beaten down by his own negative mindset.

This young child, he thought, *has shown bravery in further risking her life, and risking never seeing her family again, in the hopes of finding us, so we can still succeed in our mission of finding and freeing her family. And now, because of her willingness to step out and risk failure in finding help, she now has hope in rescuing her family, and I in rescuing my squad mates.*

Cole stood and said, "I have taken a rocky path that has beaten me down, I have had many negative self-talk bricks dropped on me emotionally, and I have cowered in the face of it all. But you have taken great risk and shown me there is hope. We will find help and rescue your family and my friends. We will succeed."

Private Cole took the child's hand and led her, and himself, out of the dark recesses of their current dungeon of a home, and together they risked everything once again to regroup with the Allies and save all those trapped and persecuted by evil.

SUCCEED WITH CHARACTER

"There are no secrets to success. It is the result of preparation, hard work, and learning from failure."[1]
– Colin Powell

As entrepreneurs—just like individuals chasing a dream, a goal, their version of success—we must be willing to lead in our journey; because no one will care as much about our dream as we do.

As leaders, it will be our responsibility to stay focused on the vision, the goal, the dream, the idea of success, and to motivate and inspire our daily lives and the work of others, helping them to keep the focus. This focus will then be to direct the hard work put into achieving such success, to, hopefully, make sure that energy, time, and resources are not used to chase every distraction that comes our way. With hard work come tough decisions necessary to inspire all that are involved, to stay on track and move toward the desired end goal, for the dream of

---

success to become reality. With each decision, we will be taking great risk with the mental, physical, spiritual, and financial stability of our own selves, our family, and all those who are helping. With each risk, we must face any fear or doubt we might encounter when it comes to success or failure.

When we face fear and doubt, we must remember the qualities of a true leader and fall back on those, which also help in the creation of a good character. Then, when we build those characteristics in ourselves, we will see the entrepreneurial journey of friendship, blessing, and generosity, which will inspire us once again to continue the cycle of focused hard work, decision making (to better ourselves and others), risk (to improve our lives and the lives of others), and the willingness to step out and face any and all failure to achieve our success; to continue serving and better our own lives, and the lives of our friends, family, and strangers—to build a better, stronger, and more prosperous life, community, nation, and world.

NOTES

CHAPTER 1

PROLOGUE

1. "Naveen Jain Quotes." BrainyQuote.com. BrainyMedia Inc, 2021. 16 January 2021. https://www.brainyquote.com/quotes/naveen_jain_822369

2. Dahl, Danielle. "50 Braveheart Quotes to Help Find Your Freedom." *Everyday Power*, 6 Apr. 2020, everydaypower.com/braveheart-quotes/.

3. "Entrepreneur." *Merriam-Webster.com*. Merriam-Webster, 2019. Web. 17 February 2019.

4. "Audrey Hepburn Quotes." BrainyQuote.com. BrainyMedia Inc, 2019. 28 July 2019. https://www.brainyquote.com/quotes/audrey_hepburn_126745

5. "The Works of the Reverend John Wesley, A. M : Wesley, John, 1703-1791: Free Download, Borrow, and Streaming." *Internet Archive*, New York: J. Emory and B. Waugh, for the Methodist Episcopal Church, J. Collard, Printer, 1 Jan. 1970, archive.org/details/03553688.1116.emory.edu/page/n1.

CHAPTER 2

AM I WORTH IT?

1. "Chris Gardner Quotes." BrainyQuote.com. BrainyMedia Inc, 2021. 16 January 2021. https://www.brainyquote.com/quotes/chris_gardner_961927

2. "Rewarding." *Merriam-Webster.com*. Merriam-Webster, 2019. Web. 17 February 2019.

3. Jones, Josh C. *Destiny: Life or Death Choose Your Destiny*. Sand Springs, OK, Bold Truth Publishing, 2020.

4. Kubrick, Stanley, director. *Stanley Kubrick's The Shining*. Warner Home Video, 2008.

5. Thomas, Damien. "30 Inspirational John Wooden Quotes." *Yourpositiveoasis.com*, yourpositiveoasis.com/30-inspirational-john-wooden-quotes/.

CHAPTER 3

LEADERSHIP

1. *The Holy Bible, New International Version*. Grand Rapids: Zondervan House, 1984. Print.

2. "Simon Sinek Quotes." BrainyQuote.com. BrainyMedia Inc, 2019. 28 July 2019. https://www.brainyquote.com/quotes/simon_sinek_568152

3. "Ben Goldacre Quotes." BrainyQuote.com. BrainyMedia Inc, 2019. 28 July 2019. https://www.brainyquote.com/quotes/ben_goldacre_552822

4. "Ronald Reagan Quotes." BrainyQuote.com. BrainyMedia Inc, 2019. 28 July 2019. https://www.brainyquote.com/quotes/ronald_reagan_183758

5. "Jack Welch Quotes." BrainyQuote.com. BrainyMedia Inc, 2019. 28 July 2019. https://www.brainyquote.com/quotes/jack_welch_833427

6. Olson, Bruce. *Bruchko*. Lake Mary, Fla: Charisma House, 2006. Print.

CHAPTER 4

HARD WORKER

1. "Thomas A. Edison Quotes." BrainyQuote.com. BrainyMedia Inc, 2021. 17 January 2021. https://www.brainyquote.com/quotes/thomas_a_edison_131293

2. Meah, Asad. "24 Motivational Sacrifice Quotes." *AwakenTheGreatnessWithin*, 26 July 2016, www.awakenthegreatnesswithin.com/24-motivational-sacrifice-quotes/.

3. "Home." *Rick's Riches*, 20 Apr. 2019, ricksriches.com/.

4. *Up in Smoke*. Dir. Lou Adler. Paramount Pictures, 1978. Film.

CHAPTER 5

DECISION MAKER

1. "Decision Making Quotes (507 Quotes)." *Goodreads*, Goodreads, www.goodreads.com/quotes/tag/ decision-making.

2. McCord, Sara. "Make Better Snap Decisions With These 4 Simple Steps." *Inc.com*, Inc., 17 Apr. 2017, www.inc.com/the-muse/make-better-snap-decisions-4-simple-steps.html.

3. Story Adapted from: "Would You Make a Popular Decision over a Right Decision?" *Managewell.net*, 5 July 2009, managewell.net/?p=607.

CHAPTER 6

RISK-TAKER

1. "Geena Davis Quotes." BrainyQuote.com. BrainyMedia Inc, 2021. 18 January 2021. https://www.brainyquote.com/quotes/ geena_davis_371447.

2. *The Holy Bible, New International Version.* Grand Rapids: Zondervan House, 1984. Print.

3. Kipling, Rudyard. "If- by Rudyard Kipling." *Poetry Foundation*, Poetry Foundation, www.poetryfoundation.org/ poems/46473/if---.

CHAPTER 7

SUCCEED & FAIL

1. "Dale Carnegie Quotes." BrainyQuote.com. BrainyMedia Inc, 2021. 18 January 2021. https://www.brainyquote.com/quotes/dale_carnegie_108922

2. M, Mateusz. "20 Empowering Les Brown Quotes." *Mateusz M*, 5 May 2016, www.mateuszm.com/15-empowering-les-brown-quotes/.

3. "Creativity." *Merriam-Webster.com*. Merriam-Webster, 2019. Web. 15 May 2019.

4. Hendry, Erica R. "7 Epic Fails Brought to You By the Genius Mind of Thomas Edison." *Smithsonian.com*, Smithsonian Institution, 20 Nov. 2013, www.smithsonianmag.com/innovation/7-epic-fails-brought-to-you-by-the-genius-mind-of-thomas-edison-180947786/.

5. M, Mateusz. "20 Empowering Les Brown Quotes." *Mateusz M*, 5 May 2016, www.mateuszm.com/15-empowering-les-brown-quotes/.

6. Fabrega, Marelisa. "You Must Be Willing to Fail to Be Creative and Innovate." *Daring to Live Fully*, 14 Oct. 2017, daringtolivefully.com/willing-to-fail.

7. Wilkinson, Bruce, David Kopp, and Heather H. Kopp. *The Dream Giver*. Sisters, OR: Multnomah Publishers, 2003. Print.

CHAPTER 8

SUCCEED WITH CHARACTER

1. "Colin Powell Quotes." BrainyQuote.com. BrainyMedia Inc, 2019. 28 July 2019. https://www.brainyquote.com/quotes/colin_powell_121363

For more information or to order copies of this book,

visit the Josh C. Jones author page at

www.bushpublishing.com

ABOUT THE AUTHOR

Josh C. Jones is the author of the well-received book *Destiny: Life or Death, Choose Your Destiny*, which his first publisher (Aaron Jones, who is in Heaven now) had said he believed to be up there with Napoleon Hill and would be, in time, the next motivational literature hit.

Josh is an entrepreneur, helping to start and run two small businesses, working years as a sole proprietor (freelance media contractor), and creating the title of "podcaster" for himself (*From My Standpoint* podcast). He has been nominated and won awards for theater and filmmaking. And he has stepped out, working in various fields, increasing his experiences and understanding, and taking the great risk to be a published author.

Josh is a Cum Laude graduate from Oral Roberts University with a bachelor's degree in media.

Josh has experience in each of the chapters he speaks of in this book, and he, just like all of us, has and will continue to take that journey to continue to build these characteristics in his life.

Josh has a goal to bring The Truth, better understanding, hope, common sense, logic, and entertainment to people through his writings and creativity; he hopes to be able to change the perspective for a better understanding.